ATTAI CHEN
ALL THE WORLD'S A STAGE

CONTENTS

5 *Glenn Adamson*
SMALL WORLDS, AFTER ALL

9 TERRA MUTANTICA

20 *Sool Park*
CORDYCEPS

21 CORDYCEPS SURVIVORS

32 MATTER OF PERSPECTIVE

50 *Sool Park*
SILENT DOWNFALLS, ALWAYS GAZING UPWARD

51 DIORAMAS

82 PRAYER NUTS

96 GERMAN TEXTS

102 *Attai Chen*
CV

Glenn Adamson
SMALL WORLDS, AFTER ALL

Stop reading. Look up from the page. What do you see? The interior of a room, probably, its various lines of ceiling, walls, and floor converging. Or, if you happen to be outside, then a landscape, receding to the horizon. The things in view diminish with distance, along a sliding scale of scale itself.

Now, a question: who taught any of us to see this way? In terms of perspective, that is, and vanishing points, and horizons, and relative scale. All of these concepts seem so natural to us, so self-evident. Yet if we look at the art of most places and times, whether prehistoric or medieval, Chinese or Mayan, we do not see such pictorial devices. Space is instead conjured in other ways, sometimes accumulated into a density, sometimes floating free, across a range of visual effects as various as human societies. This suggests a truth as perplexing as it is seemingly undeniable: vision is a culturally specific phenomenon, and the means we use to represent what we see are technologies, as artificial as any machine. There is nothing self-evident or inevitable about them.

This, at any rate, is what Erwin Panofsky thought. In a short book called *Perspective as Symbolic Form* (1924), he retraced the course of European art history from the vantage point of, well, vantage points. He argued that methods of representation closely tracked other contemporaneous branches of thought, such as mathematics and philosophy. The 14th century, he thought, marked a crucial inflection point; this was when artists like Duccio and Giotto began conceptualizing their paintings not as sacred icons, objects to embellish, but as transparent windows on the world. As Panofsky put it, they set the *disjecta membra* [disjoined fragments] of Gothic space into a new unity.[1] Gradually, this became a dominant way of showing, and hence seeing, the world. The new "general projective geometry" was a momentous shift in humanity's sense of itself, "as much a consolidation and systematization of the external world, as an extension of the domain of the self."[2]

---

1 *Erwin Panofsky, Perspective as Symbolic Form, New York 1991, p. 55.*
2 *Ibid., pp. 70 and 67-68.*

Panofsky's essay has been debated by generations of art historians, but its central contention remains persuasive: perspective had to be invented, and once it was established, it became hard to unsee it. Attai Chen showed us how. He constructed his own kind of space, free from the "perfect, synthetic, and enforced" laws of perspective. This act of self-liberation has a revolutionary aspect, analogous to contesting a restrictive political order. This may seem like a lot for jewelry to take on, but consider: the discipline is fundamentally dedicated to ornamentation, not representation. It does not show us space from an external point of view but rather supplements bodies moving *within* space, focusing and articulating our attention to them. In a sense, then, it is the perfect medium in which to explore alternative perceptual universes. Spatially speaking, jewelry is unclaimed territory: a context for experimentation that is already liberated, in a way that painting, with its overdetermined histories, could never be.

It's with these heady thoughts in mind that we can turn to Chen's recent creative trajectory, which began in 2016 with his series *Matter of Perspective* (2016). Materially, these pieces are continuous with his previous oeuvre, in that they are constructed primarily from small shards of paper. The title and predominantly lens-like format of the works, however, indicate a new preoccupation with vision. The pieces Chen had been making previously had been something like personal relics. Made of weathered, scavenged remnants, they bear titles like *Forgotten Things* and *Forgive Me Father, For I Have Sinned*. Oftentimes, they gravitated toward a Judeo-Christian iconography, fleetingly suggesting pieces of the True Cross, or saint's bones. These allusions suggested a devilish play with faith and fraudulence, prompting the thought that long before Duchamp conceived the Readymade, the church was appropriating its own found objects.

The pieces in *Matter of Perspective* are crisper and cooler in affect. Chen recalled wanting to "impose order on the chaos" that had characterized his practice up until then. The works are made mainly of tiny prisms, arranged in closed ranks and executed in a subtle grisaille palette. They somewhat resemble crystalline geological formations, with textures that feel not so much made as mined. What chiefly interested Chen in making these works, however, were their internal vectors, the shifting dynamics that they contained. Let your eye wander across their restless surfaces and you'll see what he was after. You'll find yourself settling into one pocket of space only to be dislodged, sliding headlong into another. In photographic reproduction, the pieces can even be difficult to read, with convexity and concavity flipping into one another.

It is remarkable that Chen was able to summon such a vertiginous perceptual experience in such a small physical space. At the same time, he wanted to disrupt even this unstable matrix. Some of the works include directional protrusions, transgressing their own elliptical boundaries. There are also pieces in the collection that are totally free-form, blossoming like flowers, crisscrossing like city streets, jutting upwards like skyscrapers. Chen embraced such metaphors even as he searched for internal contradiction, introducing passages that seem to inhabit contrasting, or even totally unrelated, spatial conditions.

For his last body of work, Chen looked closely at Italian art of the *trecento*, the same period that Panofsky identified as a turning point. What captivated him about this moment in art history was not the arrival of perspective but, on the contrary, the older, medieval features that were still present—what Panofsky called *disjecta membra*. He was particularly intrigued by narrative paintings in which multiple temporalities—various events in the life of a saint, for example—were represented in a single visual field. This is a curiously contemporary manner of organizing space and time, conforming to the postmodern tendency toward simultaneous and non-sequential, rather than linear, history. (This was the premise, for example, of *The Forever Now*, a 2014 exhibition of contemporary paintings at the Museum of Modern Art.) Early Renaissance art was rooted in an ideology that most people, today, would find quite alien: a dogmatically instructive means of storytelling, leaving no space for doubt. In this sense, it is the direct opposite of Chen's exploratory, open-ended approach. Yet it was still, as he put it, "an associative patchwork, a self-organized system of different timeframes," and for this reason, a powerfully suggestive source for his art.

All this looking and thinking culminated in a body of work with the collective title *All the World's a Stage*. The phrase is from Shakespeare, of course (*As You Like It*, Act II, Scene VII), and it signals an extrovert theatricality, oscillating in tone between the comedic and the tragic. Color is back in this series, the gray tones of *Matter of*

Perspective yielding to an exuberant palette. Yet the pieces can also be read as dystopian: ruinous cityscapes, collapsed buildings, billowing smoke. They were made in the shadow not only of the Covid pandemic but also of ongoing conflict in Gaza and Syria, and the horrific explosion that engulfed downtown Beirut in August of 2020. More recently still, Chen's native country of Israel has entered a period of unprecedented right-wing rule. He had no desire to keep any of this contemporary history at bay. An existential unsettlement had entered the work; still today, after his passing, it convulses with the shock of the now.

It is in this context that Chen's refusal of perspectival clarity takes on its true significance. For it is not only art historical precedence that he was out to challenge but that of his own discipline, jewelry's status as an emblematic medium, symbolic of its wearer's taste and sense of self. Chen, seeking a pervasive contingency, embraced the theater—and specifically, the plays of Shakespeare, with their gleeful gamesmanship concerning personal identity—as a working premise. The stage offers itself as a master metaphor. Like "all the men and women merely players" of *As You Like It*, his pieces "have their exits and entrances." They act out the *idea* of space, rather than simply depicting it. Individual motifs within the pieces serve much like the props in a modernist production (like the ones that Isamu Noguchi made for the choreographer Martha Graham, for example), in that they are totally open to interpretation. An amorphous wisp of grass-green might be read as an olive tree, a running river, or a patch of algae. A patch of blue and white could be an ocean wave or a broken bit of porcelain. Scale too is uncertain, so that one and the same piece can suggest a clod of earth or a whole mountain range.

Turn any of these pieces over and the sense of metamorphosis is suddenly arrested. Whatever wizardly legerdemain may be happening on the front, the back is absolutely undisguised, literal, a practical infrastructure exposed to inspection. The experience is much like stepping backstage at a theater. (It may be relevant that Chen's father worked as a stage designer in Israeli film, theater, and TV production.) These *recto* faces also call to mind the early

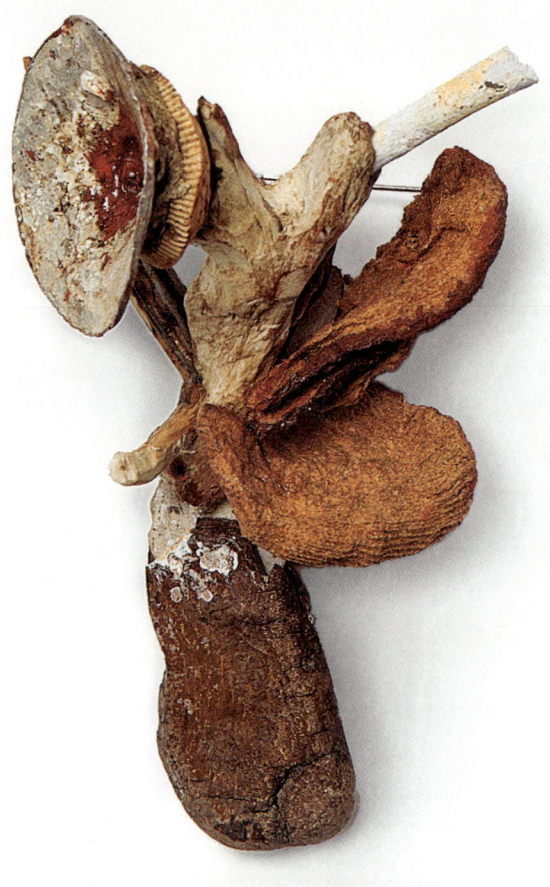

Inheritance | Brooch | 2013 | Wood, paint, silver, plastic, stainless steel, brass, aluminum | 120 × 80 × 50 mm

Jesus Superstar | Necklace | 2013 | Wood, paint, plastic, gold leaf | 400 × 75 × 50 mm

Untitled | Brooches | 2013–14 | Wood, paint, silver, stainless steel, brass, enamel, aluminum, gold leaf, butterfly, plastic | 100 × 30 × 20 mm – 80 × 35 × 25 mm

---

work of that supremely theatrical artist Robert Rauschenberg, whose *Combines* were once memorably compared by critic Leo Steinberg to the flatbed of a truck, a "receptor surface on which objects are scattered, on which data is entered, on which information may be received, printed, impressed—whether coherently or in confusion."[3] That description rings true of Chen's work, too. By releasing himself from the artifice of perspective, he allowed a different kind of reality to pour in.

Samuel Johnson once remarked of John Milton, Shakespeare's successor as England's preeminent poet, that he was "a genius that could cut a colossus from a rock, but could not carve heads upon cherry stones."[4] Chen was the other way around. The pandemic era did see him making work of unusually large size—notably, a three-meter-wide wall sculpture, shown at Antonella Villanova Gallery in his exhibition *Pars Pro Toto* ("the part standing for the whole"). But like most jewelers, he was essentially a miniaturist, a devotee of the art of compression. This is abundantly apparent in a subgroup of pieces in *All the World's a Stage*, which extend his earlier lens-like compositions into a hemispherical format. They were inspired by yet another art historical source: carved boxwood "prayer nuts," which were made primarily in the Netherlands, in the sixteenth century. It's not surprising that Chen should admire these extraordinarily intricate objects. They not only are marvels of skill but also show just how much space can be forced into a small, non-perspectival volume, tumbling around like clothes in a dryer. What particularly astonishes is the impression of vast distance that the woodcarvers conjured, a trick that Chen also mastered. We are in the domain of the diorama, here, where the magic of representation calls conspicuous attention to itself.

---

3 Leo Steinberg, "Other Criteria: The Flatbed Picture Plane," in Other Criteria: Confrontations with Twentieth-Century Art, New York 1972, p. 84.
4 Samuel Johnson quoted in Boswell's Life of Johnson, vol. 2: 1776–1784, London et al. 1904, p. 559.

Ole-Bebo | Necklace | 2014 | Wood, paint, silver, plastic, brass, fabric, gold | 380 × 300 × 80 mm

TERRA MUTANTICA

Untitled | Necklace | 2015 | Wood, paper, paint, silver | 190 × 92 × 43 mm

Where does it all deposit us? A clue comes via one of Chen's favorite books, David Hockney's *Secret Knowledge* (2001), which has been as influential a re-scripting of art history in our own time as Panofsky's *Perspective as Symbolic Form* was in his (the two texts are profitably read in parallel). Hockney mounts a convincing case that paradigm shifts in representation—the sudden, mesmerizing verisimilitude that arose in Dutch painting in the seventeenth century, for example—are usually best explained as the result of improving technology, especially *camera obscuras* and other lens-based apparatus. (Hockney explains the relative lack of documentary evidence for such devices by hypothesizing that they were closely guarded trade secrets, hence his book's title.) While Chen wasn't literally using assistive technology in this way, it is impossible to believe that his work would take the forms that it did were it not for the prevailing conditions of vision in our time, which are, of course, digital in nature. Computers see without actually looking. The internet creates the illusion that all points of reference are instantly available while also thoroughly decontextualizing them. As the artist-theorist Hito Steyerl observed in her 2011 essay "In Free Fall," a postmodern response to Panofsky's argument, the "stable and single point of view is being supplemented (and often replaced) by multiple perspectives, overlapping windows, distorted flight lines, and divergent vanishing points."[5]

Chen offered a counterpoint to this fractured, infinite sea of immaterial imagery, responding to the frictionless flow of the present—the distraction machine that we all inhabit, in which truth and falsity are inextricable entwined—with his own, equally fluid but exquisitely crafted microcosms. They are "fabrications" in every sense of that word: made up from scratch, putting on a good show, at once assertively tangible and entirely elusive. Hold one in your palm, and take a close look: what you'll see is a world nothing like our own, which nonetheless grasps it whole.

---

5 Hito Steyerl, "In Free Fall," e-flux Journal 24 (April 2011), https://www.e-flux.com/journal/24/67860/in-free-fall-a-thought-experiment-on-vertical-perspective/

Clashes | Necklace | 2014 | Wood, paint, plastic, brass, porcelain, iron, cardboard, linen | 330 × 210 × 90 mm

Sool Park
CORDYCEPS

To be born again and to give up one's current life is the old formula of immortality. On closer inspection, nature is full of immortal beings; indeed it even seems impossible to identify in it a normal mortal. A body that once moved back and forth on the forest floor comes to a standstill to be reborn. Quite unexpectedly and wonderfully, it is taken over by a stranger at the cost of its old life; in this transition it adorns and renews itself, and becomes another being. So who dies in this body and who lives? This question also applies to us, since we also inhabit a body and must constantly live in the process of becoming, like guests in a dream.

Cordyceps Survivor | Brooch | 2015 | Paper, wood, paint, silver, plastic, stainless steel | 125 × 80 × 50 mm

Untitled | Brooch | 2015 | Wood, paint, shibuichi, plastic, brass, paper, iron, enamel, stainless steel | 130 × 130 × 50 mm

Reduction | Ring | 2014 | Wood, paint, silver, plastic, paper | 100 × 70 × 70 mm

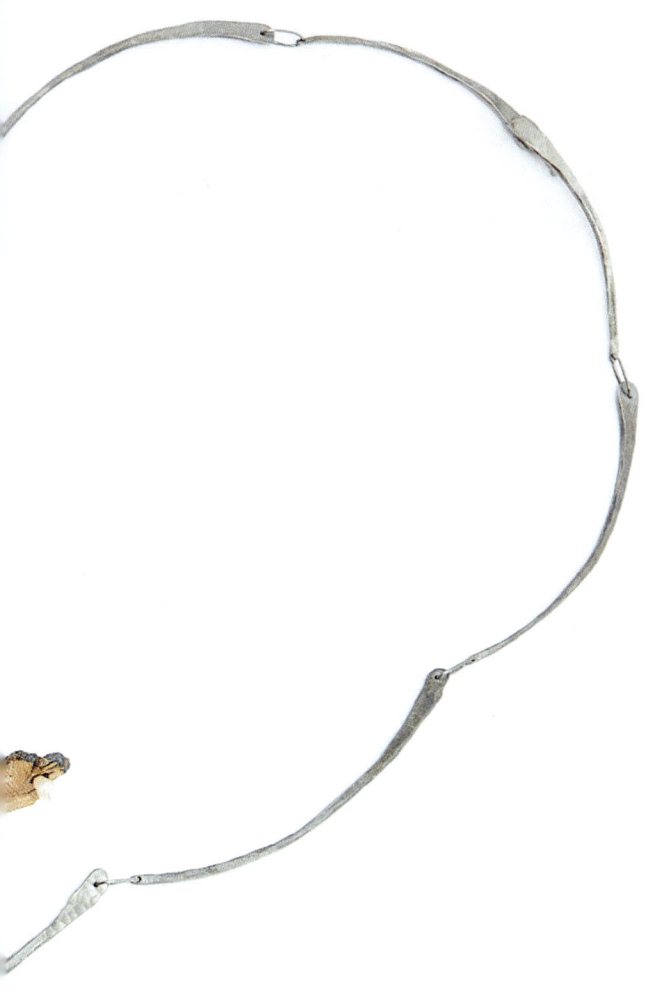

Cordyceps Survivor 4 | Neckpiece | 2018 | Wood, paper, paint, pearls, silver, plastic, nails, bio-resin, mica, flock, hair, carborundum | 180 × 75 × 50 mm

Occasional Figure Head | Brooch | 2015 | Wood, paint, silver, brass, plastic, stainless steel, copper | 180 × 180 × 70 mm

Pietà | Brooch | 2015 | Wood, paint, graphite, silver, plastic, gold, gold leaf, stainless steel, copper | 165 × 110 × 50 mm

Cordyceps Survivor 3 | Brooch | 2018 | Wood, paper, paint, pearls, silver, plastic, brass, copper, stainless steel, flock | 70 × 160 × 50 mm | Front and back

Untitled | Brooch | 2016 | Paper, paint, silver, wood, graphite, stainless steel | 80 × 65 × 25 mm

Untitled | Brooch | 2016 | Paper, paint, silver, wood, graphite, stainless steel | 92 × 75 × 45 mm

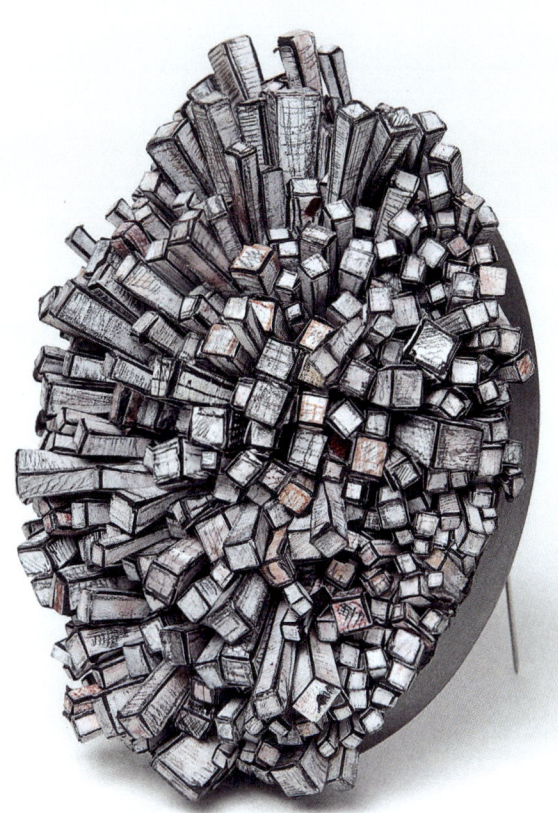

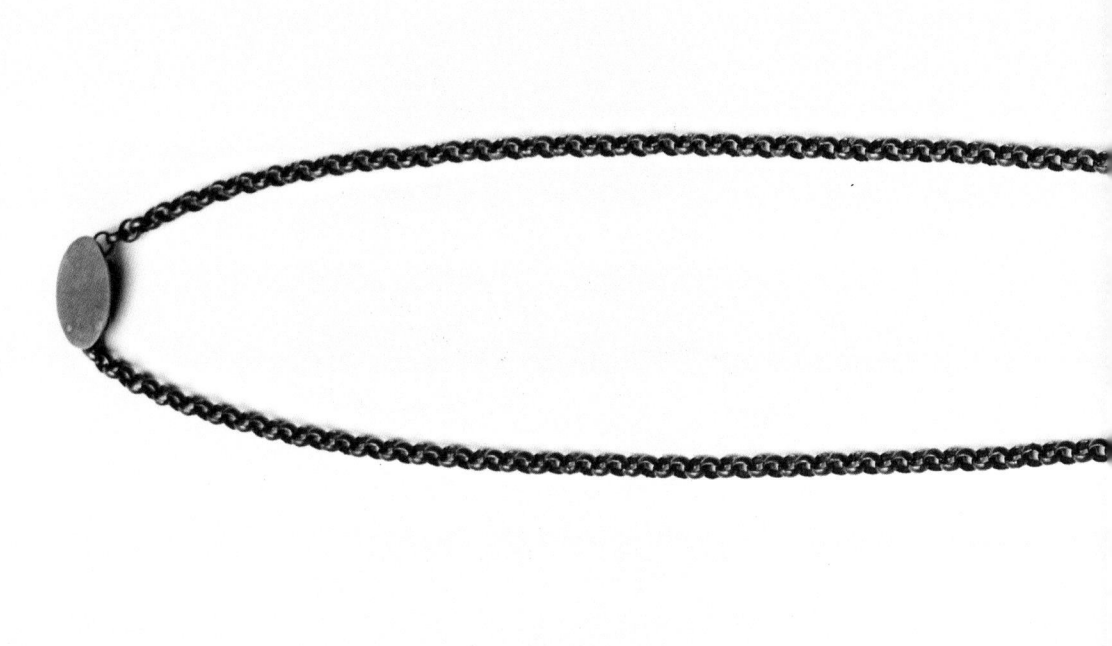

Untitled | Necklace | 2016 | Paper, paint, silver, wood, graphite | 200 × 140 × 45 mm

↑ *Untitled | Brooch | 2018 | Paper, paint, silver, wood, graphite, stainless steel | 54 × 42 × 25 mm*
→ *Untitled | Necklace | 2017 | Paper, paint, silver, wood, graphite | 300 × 350 × 35 mm*

Untitled | Necklace | 2017 | Paper, paint, silver, wood, graphite | 300 × 150 × 35 mm

Untitled | Brooch | 2020 | Paper, paint, silver, wood, graphite, stainless steel | 185 × 55 × 28 mm

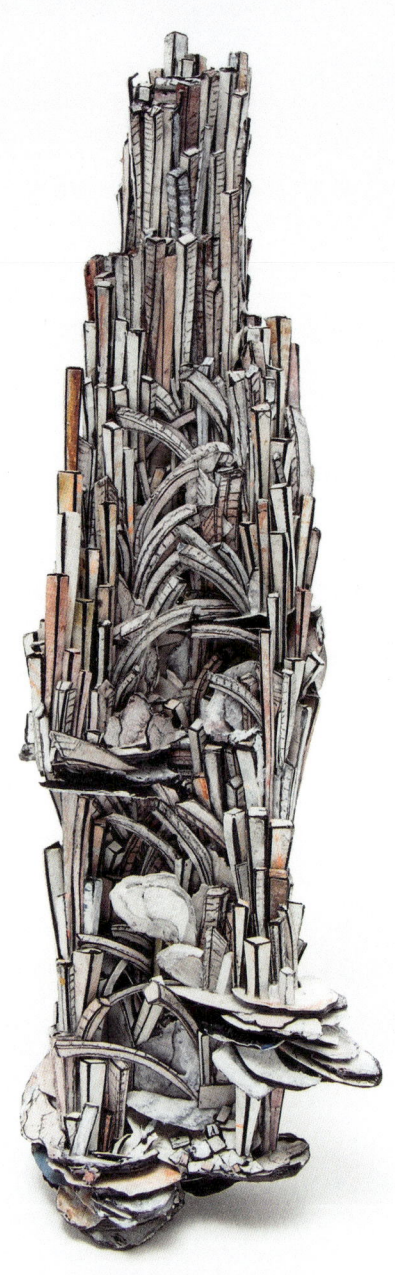

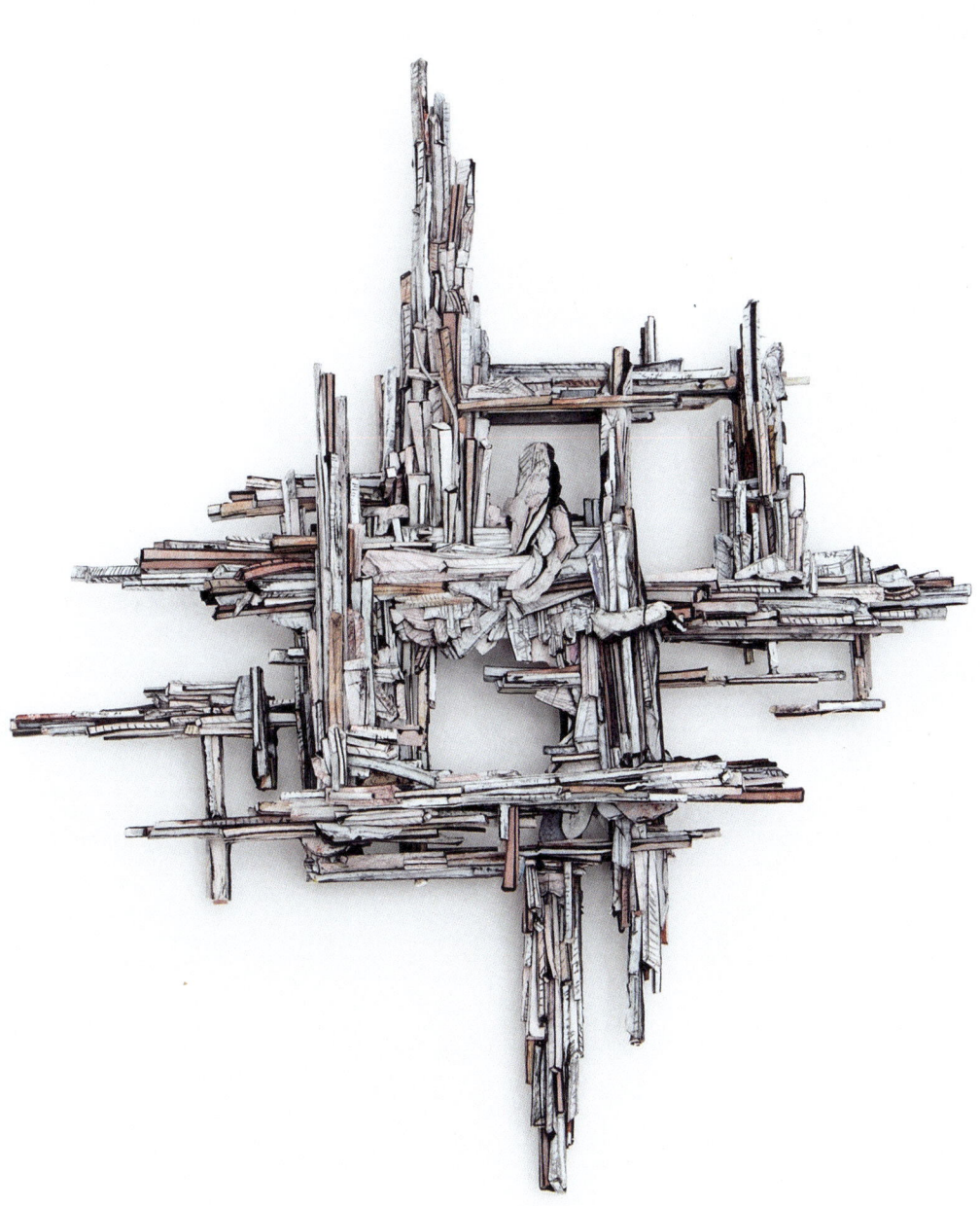

Untitled | Brooch | 2021 | Paper, paint, silver, wood, graphite, stainless steel | 150 × 180 × 25 mm

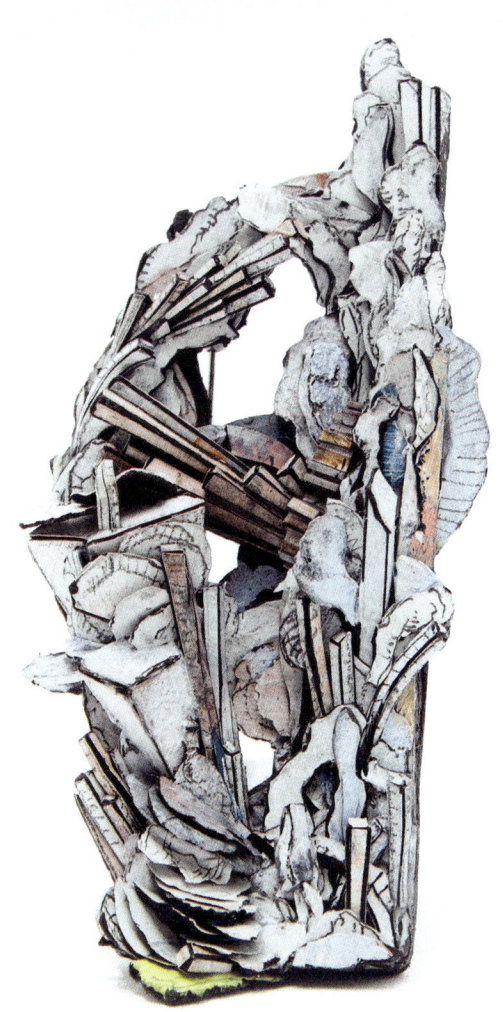

↑ Untitled | Brooch | 2020 | Paper, paint, silver, wood, graphite, stainless steel | 105 × 50 × 23 mm
← Untitled | Brooch | 2020 | Paper, paint, silver, wood, graphite, stainless steel | 115 × 69 × 30 mm | Front and back

Untitled | Brooch | 2021–23 | Paper, wood, paint, silver, stainless steel | 111 × 85 × 30 mm

Untitled | Brooch | 2020 | Paper, paint, gold leaf, silver, stainless steel | 90 × 80 × 45 mm

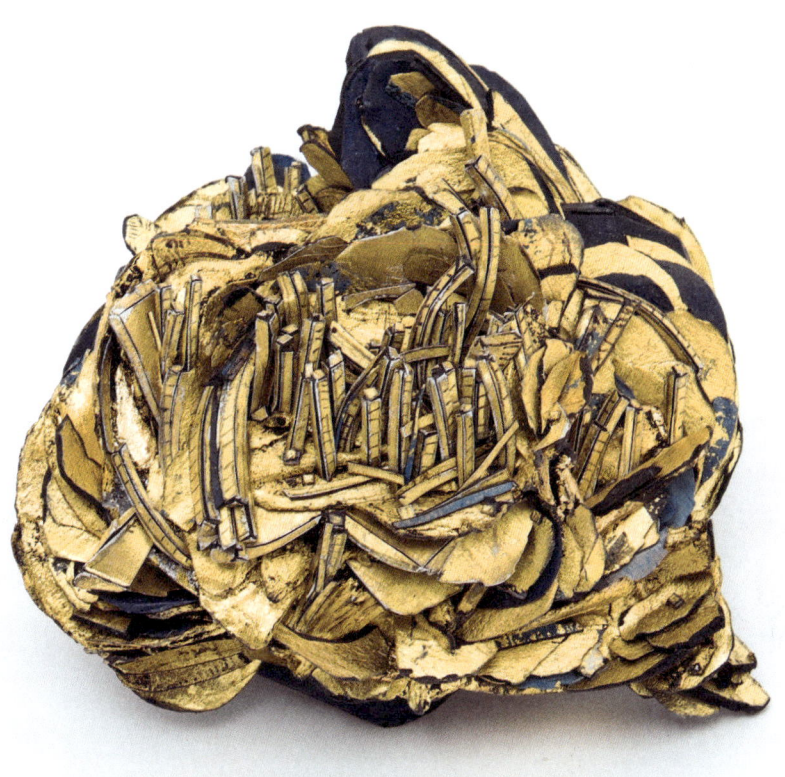

Untitled | Neckpiece | 2021 | Paper, paint, gold leaf, silver leaf, silver | 125 × 105 × 60 mm

Sool Park

SILENT DOWNFALLS, ALWAYS GAZING UPWARD

IT FILLS US. WE ARRANGE IT. IT COLLAPSES.
WE ARRANGE IT AGAIN, AND COLLAPSE OURSELVES.
Rainer Maria Rilke, The Duino Elegies (8th Elegy)

Like all optical media, our eyes refract light. What we see, therefore, is always what has been refracted, never reality in its entirety. Indeed, seeing is refracting, that is the ancient truism on which modern philosophy is premised, and so is all the talk about our only having images of things, never the things themselves. What philosophers themselves produce are, however, also merely images, that is, images of the world. On the other hand, whereas philosophy, exhausted, is gradually ceasing to project fresh world views, the men and women who are artists now seem to be the better philosophers. Usually unwittingly, they let ideas filter through in their successful works that grasp our innermost being and channel it into a new visibility. In that sense, an artwork is a "model of reality,"[1] or a microcosm.

In Attai Chen's recent works, we have two competing models for seeing: two world views that confront each other, or, one could say, two types of *stages*. One world view *(Dioramas)* is centrifugal, attesting to refraction; the second *(Prayer Nuts)* dreams, on the other hand, of concentric wholeness and regeneration. Does this represent a clash between them, or rather a compensatory relationship? Both would seem to be the case here—just as light and dark cancel each other out yet are merely two sides of *one* thing. Nietzsche, too, writes of a healing light that appears to him who has gazed too deeply into the abyss.[2] Thus the two world views are mutually evocative, just as dreams successively appear, interpret each other, and at the same time are perplexing.

---

1 Ludwig Wittgenstein, *Tractatus Logico-Philosophicus*, 2.12.
2 Friedrich Nietzsche, *Kritische Studienausgabe (Geburt der Tragödie: The Birth of Tragedy)*, vol. 1, p. 65.

Untitled | Brooch | 2021 | Wood, paint, silver, stainless steel | 140 × 110 × 55 mm

Dioramas: The world as a stage

The literal meaning of the word "diorama" comes from "what can be seen through, discerned." A diorama, therefore, looks back into spatial depth and matches a stage backdrop to what is ongoing in the foreground. In Attai Chen's *Dioramas* works this relationship between foreground and background seems, however, to have been oddly reversed. In *Untitled*, p. 70 what is going on in the foreground on water (distress at sea?) is almost unrecognizable, meaningless, in fact, whereas the elements in the background soar up hyperbolically, in almost phantasmagorically rampant overgrowth. An individual is drowning without a sound while the world is shaken to its foundations. The quasi-architectonic structure, which is collapsing from faulty design, is not all that is endangered; so, too, is reality as such: the plane farthest to the rear is a universal conflagration. It is a scene in miniature of the current global situation, in which everything is falling apart, going up in flames, or going under. This scene is, however, invested with an eerie profound stillness. Is this helplessness against the way of the world, which we are being painfully forced to learn? Is this the new apathy?

This silent disintegration is a pattern that runs through the entire *Dioramas* series. Its consistent diagnostic feature is the impossibility of stability, the recurrent infringement of its own format. Seemingly natural scenes such as *Untitled*, p. 51 harbor sinister portents; its plasticity does not make the smoke less menacing but rather reveals the staged character of what is happening. "All the world's a stage," as Shakespeare writes in *As You Like It*,[3] and suddenly we understand what is breaking down here—the "stage-like nature of the world." Façades turn out to be false fronts set up by a set designer; the prompter is caught in the act. An old suspicion is confirmed. Is this freedom? Or impossibility?

Prayer Nuts: The second world

The idea behind the medieval invention of the prayer nut was probably to create a portable universe. Attai Chen's series *Prayer Nuts* is an extension into art of this ancient idea of making material an

---

3 William Shakespeare, *As You Like It*, Act II, Scene VII.

inner refuge to counter the breakdown of meaning. It cancels the Nowhere-ness and No-oneness of the external world in an attempt "to bind the world's innermost core together."[4] Its constituents remain the architectonic and geographic elements in miniature, as in the *Dioramas* works. The menace lives on; the structures are brittle, shattered, charred, and, in any case, abandoned, even where they unexpectedly flash tints of gold. Yet all these desolate landscapes are arranged spherically around a center; the vault of Heaven is even seen to have materialized, a typical feature of religious imaginations. Optical perspective has vanished from view because reality itself is bent out of shape here to form an enclosed, delimited whole. Here is a mystical world[5] but, at the same time, the world we do in fact perceive around us. In *Untitled*, p. 89 we see a well-ordered structure that is nonetheless uninhabitable and uninhabited. Half reminiscent of Heaven, half recalling Hell, it can be read as a model of the coherence of conflicting mental states. The elements in *Untitled*, p. 93/r, on the other hand, are impossible constructs and exposed as façades, but they are securely integrated in the concentric sphere because here there is gravity, which provides stability. A crucial element of these microcosms is their *dual world* character. In them things attain the longed-for wholeness even though it is marred by grief and loss, as in *Untitled*, p. 93/l. Then in *Untitled*, p. 86/r, p. 87 a transfigured view flares up as a magical moment of regeneration.

But these counter-worlds of Attai Chen's are more than world views because they are intended to be pieces of jewelry. As such, they have been conceived to be worn on one's own body, to be felt and communicated. Could one say with Ilse Aichinger that their function is to drag the downfall in front of oneself?[6] For these are silent images of downfalls that precede one step ahead of us and say something dark. In them we see that we have broken the world with our seeing. But we also see that isn't the last of it. Because upward goes our gaze until it encompasses the blue vault of Heaven.

---

4 Johann Wolfgang von Goethe, "Night," in Faust: A Tragedy, Part I, https://www.poetryintranslation.com/PITBR/German/FaustIScenesItoIII.php
5 Ludwig Wittgenstein, Tractatus Logico-Philosophicus, 6.45: "Feeling the world as a limited whole—it is this that is mystical."
6 Ilse Aichinger, Bad Words, transl. Uljana Wolf and Christian Hawkey, London 2022, p. 69.

A Memory of Staged Reality | Wine goblet | 2016 | Wood, paper, silver, gold leaf, paint, plastic | 120 × 120 × 160 mm | Two views | Detail on pages 52–53

Untitled | Brooch | 2021–23 | Paper, paint, silver, stainless steel | 101 × 102 × 50 mm | Front and back

↑ *Untitled | Neckpiece | 2021–23 | Wood, paint, brass, silver | 150 × 110 × 85 mm*
↖ *Untitled | Brooch | 2021–23 | Wood, paint, graphite, mica, aluminum, brass, silver, stainless steel | 145 × 130 × 83 mm*
← *Untitled | Brooch | 2021–23 | Wood, paint, brass, silver, stainless steel | 120 × 116 × 73 mm*

Untitled | Neckpiece | 2021–23 | Wood, paint, paper, gold leaf, thread, plastic, aluminum, silver, stainless steel | 160 × 150 × 40 mm

↓ Untitled | Brooch | 2021–23 | Wood, paper, paint, silver, stainless steel | 125 × 105 × 42 mm
→ Untitled | Drawing | 2022 | Cardboard, acrylic, pencil | 250 × 176 mm

Untitled | Brooch | 2021–23 | Wood, paint, brass, silver, stainless steel | 130 × 60 × 43 mm | Front and back

↓ *Untitled | Brooch | 2021–23 | Paper, paint, wood, brass, silver, stainless steel | 138 × 128 × 62 mm*
← *Untitled | Drawing | 2022 | Cardboard, acrylic, pencil | 250 × 172 mm*

Untitled | Brooch | 2021–23 | Wood, paint, plastic, brass, silver, stainless steel | 159 × 90 × 42 mm | Front and back

Untitled | Brooch | 2021–23 | Wood, paint, gold leaf, graphite, aluminum, brass, silver, stainless steel | 168 × 110 × 60 mm

Untitled | Brooch | 2021–23 | Wood, paint, brass, silver, stainless steel | 142 × 94 × 75 mm | Front and back

Untitled | Brooch | 2021–23 | Wood, paint, graphite, brass, silver, stainless steel | 150 × 112 × 59 mm

↑ *Untitled | Brooch | 2021–23 | Wood, paint, sweetwater pearls, brass, silver, stainless steel | 165 × 92 × 75 mm*
↗ *Untitled | Brooch | 2021–23 | Wood, paint, paper, carborundum, plastic, brass, silver, stainless steel | 145 × 76 × 60 mm*
→ *Untitled | Brooch | 2021–23 | Paper, paint, wood, thread, silver, stainless steel | 145 × 90 × 35 mm*

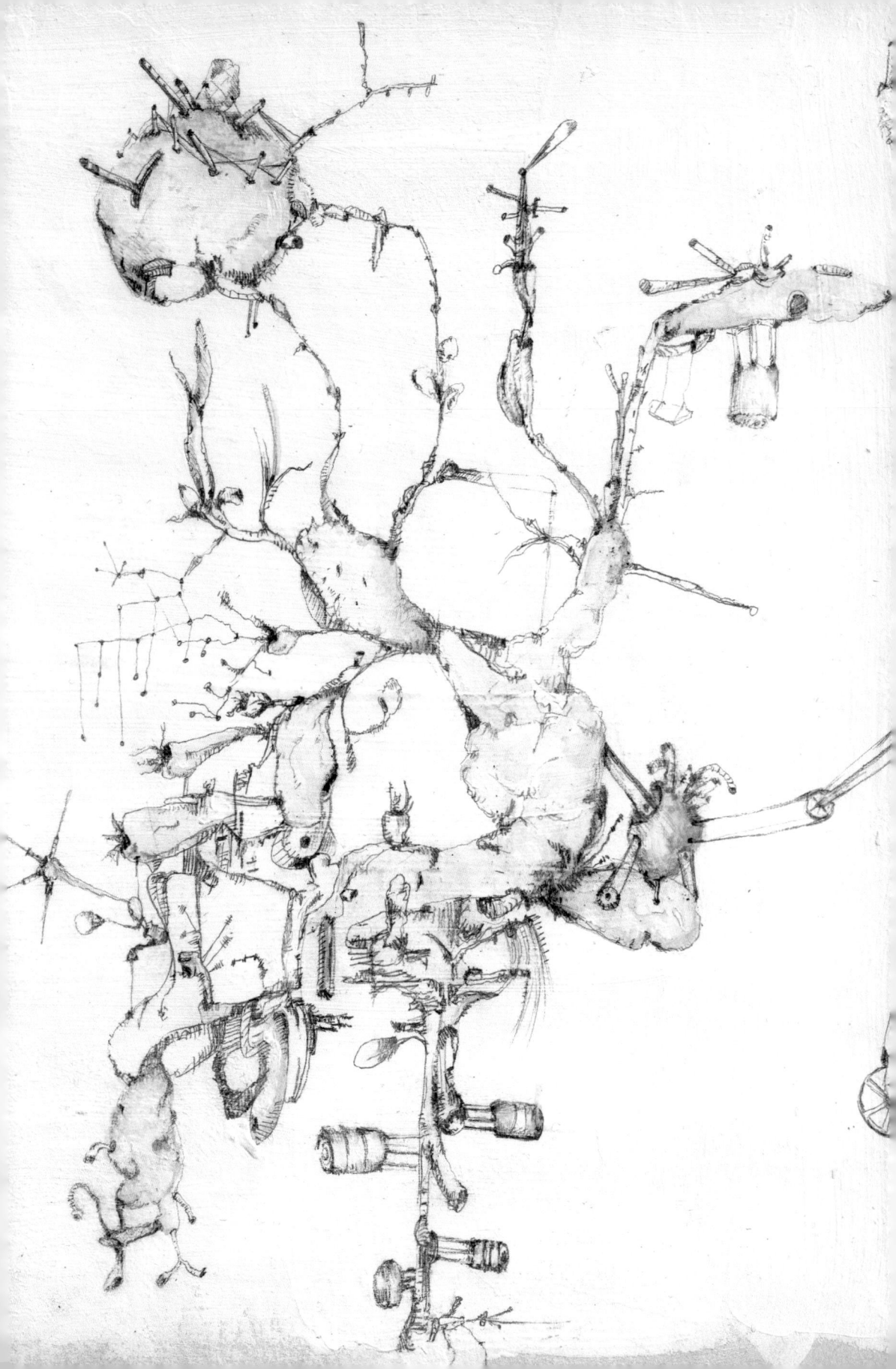

↓ *Untitled | Brooch | 2021–23 | Wood, paper, paint, carborundum, silver, stainless steel | 75 × 60 × 32 mm*
← *Untitled | Drawing | 2022 | Cardboard, acrylic, pencil | 252 × 177 mm*

← *Untitled | Pendant | 2022–23 | Wood, paper, paint, silver | 73 × 73 × 40 mm | Detail on pages 82–83*

↖ ↑ *Untitled | Pendant | 2022–23 | Paper, paint, wood, silver | 73 × 73 × 40 mm | Front and back*

↑ *Untitled | Pendant | 2022–23 | Paper, paint, plastic, silver | 72 × 72 × 36 mm*
↗ *Untitled | Pendant | 2022–23 | Paper, paint, gold leaf, sweetwater pearls, silver | 73 × 73 × 36 mm*

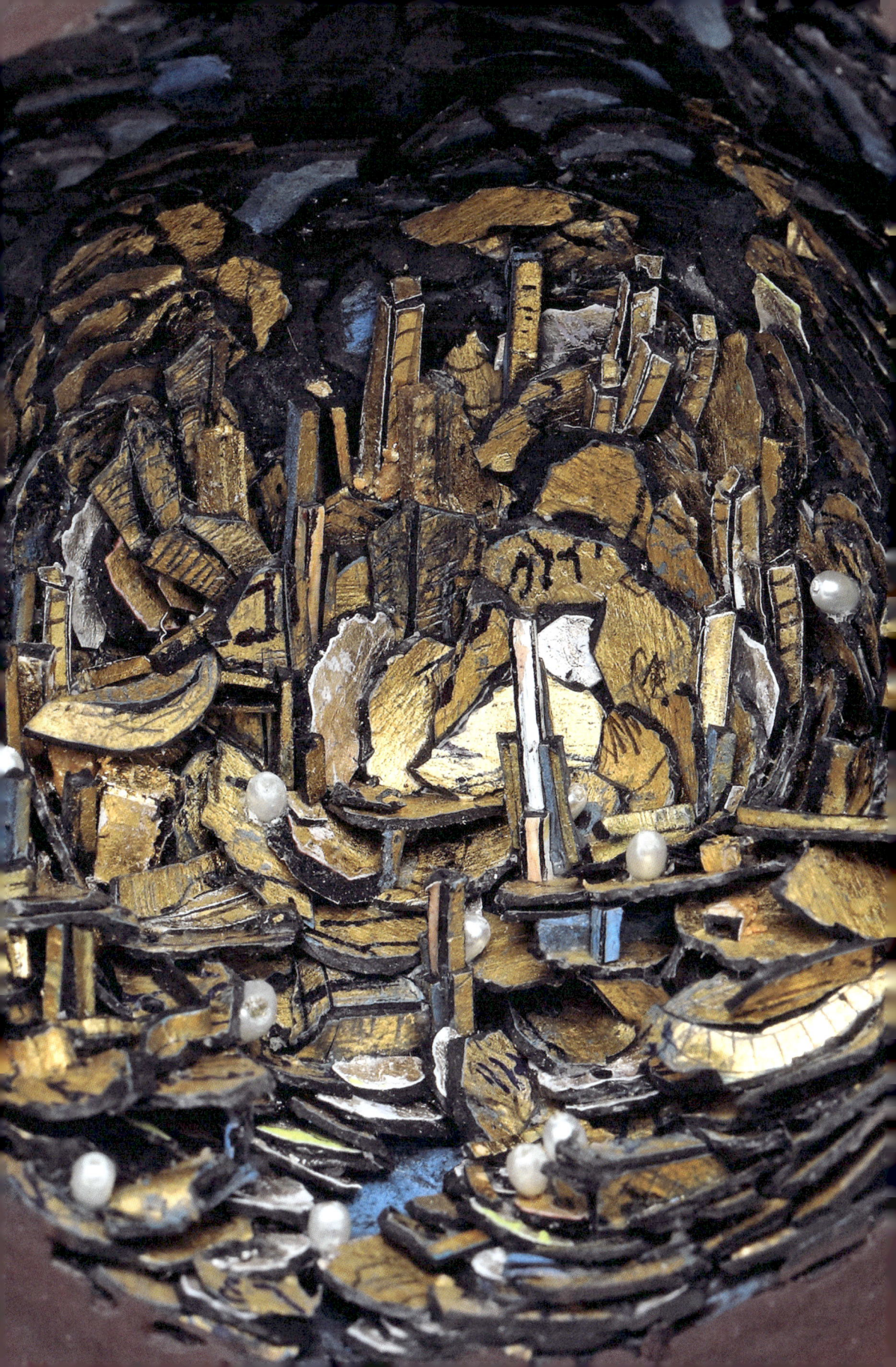

↑ *Untitled | Pendant | 2022–23 | Paper, paint, wood, gold leaf, carborundum, silver | 72 × 72 × 37 mm*
↖ *Untitled | Pendant | 2022–23 | Paper, paint, wood, silver | 63 × 63 × 32 mm*
← *Untitled | Pendant | 2022–23 | Paper, paint, wood, silver | 72 × 72 × 37 mm*

Untitled | Pendant | 2022–23 | Paper, paint, silver, brass | 62 × 62 × 35 mm

↑ Untitled | Pendant | 2022-23 | Paper, paint, silver | 71 × 71 × 35 mm
↗ Untitled | Pendant | 2022-23 | Paper, paint, wood, silver | 73 × 73 × 41 mm
→ Untitled | Pendant | 2022-23 | Paper, paint, silver | 72 × 72 × 39 mm

Untitled | Pendant | 2022-23 | Paper, paint, silver | 63 × 63 × 38 mm

Glenn Adamson
KLEINE WELTEN

Hören Sie auf zu lesen. Blicken Sie von der Seite auf. Was sehen Sie? Die Einrichtung eines Zimmers vermutlich und die konvergierenden Linien von Decke, Wänden und Fußboden. Oder, falls Sie draußen sind, eine Landschaft, die sich am Horizont verliert. Entlang einer gleitenden Maßstabsskala werden die sichtbaren Dinge mit der Entfernung kleiner.

Jetzt eine Frage: Wer hat irgendjemandem von uns beigebracht, so zu sehen? Perspektivisch also, mit Fluchtpunkten, Horizonten und relativen Maßstäben. Alle diese Begriffe erscheinen uns so natürlich, so selbstverständlich. Doch wenn wir die Kunst der allermeisten Orte und Epochen betrachten, ob prähistorisch oder mittelalterlich, ob in China oder bei den Maya, dann sehen wir diese Mittel der Darstellung nicht. Raum wird stattdessen auf andere Weise beschworen, mal durch Anhäufung verdichtet, mal im freien Fluss, mit einer Reihe von optischen Effekten, die so verschieden sind wie menschliche Gesellschaften. Die Wahrheit, die sich daraus ergibt, ist so verwirrend wie anscheinend unabweisbar: Sehen ist ein kulturspezifisches Phänomen, und die Mittel, die wir verwenden, um das Gesehene darzustellen, sind Techniken, so künstlich wie jede Maschine. Nichts an ihnen ist selbstverständlich oder naturgegeben.

So jedenfalls dachte Erwin Panofsky. In seinem Aufsatz „Die Perspektive als ‚symbolische Form'" (1924) zeichnete er den Verlauf der europäischen Kunstgeschichte aus dem Blickwinkel von, nun ja, Blickwinkeln nach. Darstellungsmethoden, so sein Argument, folgen aufs Engste den zeitgleich vorherrschenden Zweigen des Denkens, wie der Mathematik oder der Philosophie. Das 14. Jahrhundert markierte für ihn einen entscheidenden Wendepunkt – jene Zeit, da Künstler wie Duccio und Giotto anfingen, ihre Gemälde nicht mehr als sakrale Ikonen, als schmückende Objekte zu konzipieren, sondern als transparente Fenster zur Welt, in denen sich einzelne Elemente festmachen ließen, „nur daß es eben des gotischen Raumsinns bedurfte, um diese disiecta membra [zerstreuten Einzelteile] zur Einheit zusammenzuschließen."[1] Nach und nach setzte sich diese Art, die Welt zu zeigen und folglich auch zu sehen, als vorherrschend durch. Die neue „allgemeine projektive Geometrie", so Panofsky, brachte eine weitreichende Veränderung in der Selbstwahrnehmung des Menschen mit sich: Sie war „ebensowohl als Befestigung und Systematisierung der Außenwelt, wie als Erweiterung der Ichsphäre"[2] zu verstehen.

Seit Generationen debattiert die Kunstgeschichte über Panofskys Abhandlung, deren zentrale Behauptung jedoch bis heute überzeugt: Die Perspektive musste erst erfunden werden, und nachdem sie eingeführt war, wurde es schwierig, sie ungesehen zu machen. Attai Chen zeigte uns, wie es geht. Er konstruierte seine eigenen Räume, frei von den „perfekten, künstlichen und erzwungenen" Gesetzen der Perspektive. Dieser Akt der Selbstbefreiung hat etwas Revolutionäres an sich, vergleichbar mit der Infragestellung einer restriktiven politischen Ordnung. Das mag für Schmuckstücke wie eine große Aufgabe erscheinen, doch bedenken wir, dass Schmuck grundsätzlich der Verzierung gewidmet ist, nicht der Darstellung. Er zeigt uns den Raum nicht von außen, sondern ergänzt vielmehr Körper, die sich *im* Raum bewegen, er fokussiert und formuliert unsere auf sie gerichtete Aufmerksamkeit. Darum ist er in gewisser Hinsicht das perfekte Medium, um alternative Wahrnehmungswelten zu erforschen. Räumlich gesprochen ist Schmuck unbeanspruchtes Terrain: ein Kontext für Experimente, der bereits befreit ist – und zwar auf eine Weise, wie es die Malerei mit ihrer überbestimmten Geschichte niemals sein könnte.

---

1 Erwin Panofsky, „Perspektive als ‚symbolische Form'", in: Aufsätze zu Grundfragen der Kunstwissenschaft, Berlin 1980, S. 116.
2 Ebd., S. 125 und 123.

Mit diesen hochfliegenden Gedanken im Sinn können wir uns Chens neuester kreativer Entwicklungskurve zuwenden, die 2016 mit der Serie *Matter of Perspective* begann. Materiell knüpfen diese Stücke insofern an seine bisherige Arbeit an, als sie überwiegend aus kleinen Papierschnipseln entstanden sind. Der Name und das mehrheitlich linsenförmige Format der Arbeiten lassen jedoch auf eine neue Beschäftigung mit dem Sehen schließen. Chens frühere Stücke waren so etwas wie persönliche Relikte. Aus verwitterten, zusammengesuchten Resten gefertigt, trugen sie Titel wie *Forgotten Things* oder *Forgive Me Father, For I Have Sinned*. Oftmals tendierten sie zu einer jüdisch-christlichen Ikonografie und deuteten flüchtig auf Partikel des Heiligen Kreuzes oder Knochenstücke von Heiligen hin. Diese Andeutungen suggerierten ein teuflisches Spiel zwischen Glaube und Betrügerei und legten den Verdacht nahe, dass sich die Kirche ihre eigenen Fundstücke schon aneignete, lange bevor Marcel Duchamp das Readymade erfand.

Die Stücke aus der Serie *Matter of Perspective* wirken emotional klarer und kühler. Wie Chen sich erinnerte, wollte er „Ordnung in das Chaos bringen", das seine Praxis bis dahin geprägt hatte. Die Arbeiten bestehen hauptsächlich aus winzigen, dicht zusammengedrängten und in feiner Grisaille-Palette ausgeführten Prismen. Mit ihren eher natürlich als künstlich hergestellt wirkenden Texturen erinnern sie ein wenig an kristalline geologische Formationen. Was Chen bei der Anfertigung dieser Arbeiten jedoch vor allem interessierte, waren ihre inneren Vektoren, war die veränderliche Dynamik, die sie beinhalten. Lassen Sie Ihren Blick über die unruhigen Oberflächen wandern, und Sie werden erkennen, worauf er aus war. Kaum haben Sie sich in einer Ecke räumlich eingerichtet, werden Sie daraus vertrieben und schlittern kopfüber in die nächste. Auf Fotografien sind die Stücke bisweilen sogar schwer zu lesen, weil Konvexität und Konkavität ineinander übergehen.

Bemerkenswert ist, dass Chen auf einem so kleinen Raum so schwindelerregende Sinneserfahrungen unterbringen konnte. Gleichzeitig wollte er sogar diese instabilen Strukturen noch aufbrechen. Einige Arbeiten weisen gezielte Vorsprünge auf, die sich über die vorgegebenen elliptischen Grenzen hinwegsetzen. Andere Stücke in der Sammlung sind vollkommen frei gestaltet, blühen wie Blumen, verlaufen kreuz und quer wie ein Straßennetz in der Stadt, ragen in die Höhe wie Wolkenkratzer. Chen nutzte solche Metaphern, während er nach inneren Widersprüchen suchte, und versah seine Stücke mit Passagen, die in gegensätzlichen oder sogar vollkommen unverbundenen räumlichen Bedingungen nebeneinander zu existieren scheinen.

Er begann, die italienische Kunst des Trecento zu studieren, desselben Zeitraums, den Panofsky als Wendepunkt identifiziert hatte. Was Chen an diesem Augenblick der Kunstgeschichte faszinierte, war nicht die Einführung der Perspektive. Im Gegenteil, ihm ging es um die älteren, die mittelalterlichen Merkmale, die noch vorhanden sind – um das, was Panofsky als „disiecta membra" bezeichnete. Ihn beeindruckte vor allem die erzählende Malerei, in der ein einzelnes Werk mehrere Zeitlichkeiten umfasst – etwa verschiedene Ereignisse im Leben eines Heiligen. Diese seltsam moderne Art und Weise, Raum und Zeit zu organisieren, entspricht der postmodernen Neigung zur gleichzeitigen und nichtlinearen Geschichte anstelle einer chronologischen Geschichtsschreibung. (2014 zum Beispiel diente diese Zeitlosigkeit als Ausgangspunkt für *The Forever Now*, eine Ausstellung zeitgenössischer Malerei im Museum of Modern Art in New York.) Die Kunst der Frührenaissance wurzelte in einer Ideologie, von der die meisten Menschen heutzutage befremdet wären: Kunst galt als dogmatisch belehrendes Mittel des Geschichtenerzählens, das keinen Raum für Zweifel ließ. Insofern ist sie das genaue Gegenteil der forschenden, ergebnisoffenen Arbeitsweise von Attai Chen – aber auch, wie er es ausdrückte, „ein assoziativer Flickenteppich, ein selbstorganisiertes System unterschiedlicher Zeitrahmen" und darum als Quelle für sein künstlerisches Schaffen außerordentlich anregend.

All dieses Sehen und Denken gipfelte in einer neuen Werkgruppe, die von Chen den übergeordneten Titel *All the World's a Stage* (Die ganze Welt ist [eine] Bühne) erhielt. Der Ausspruch stammt natürlich von William Shakespeare (*Wie es euch gefällt*, Akt 2, Szene 7) und signalisiert eine extrovertierte Theatralik, die im Ton zwischen komödiantisch und tragisch oszilliert. Die Farbe ist in dieser Serie zurück, die Grautöne von *Matter of Perspective* haben einer überschäumenden Palette Platz gemacht. Gleichzeitig lassen sich die Stücke auch als dystopisch interpretieren: verfallene Stadtlandschaften, eingestürzte Häuser, Rauchschwaden. Sie sind nicht nur im Schatten der Coronapandemie, sondern auch vor dem Hintergrund der anhaltenden Konflikte in Syrien und im Gazastreifen sowie der verheerenden Explosion im Hafen von Beirut entstanden, die im August 2020 auch Teile der Beiruter Innenstadt verwüstete. In noch jüngerer Zeit begann in Chens Heimatland Israel eine Phase rechter Regierungsmacht, wie man sie bis dato nicht kannte. Chen selbst verspürte kein Verlangen, sich irgendeinen Teil dieser Gegenwartsgeschichte vom Leib zu halten. Eine existenzielle Unruhe war in sein Werk eingezogen; noch heute, nach seinem Tod, erbebt es unter dem Schock des Moments.

Erst in diesem Kontext nimmt Chens Absage an die perspektivische Eindeutigkeit ihre wahre Dimension an. Denn er wollte nicht nur die kunsthistorische Tradition herausfordern, sondern auch die Vorbilder seines eigenen Fachs, den Status von Schmuck als emblematisches Medium, als Symbol für Geschmack und Selbstempfinden seiner Trägerinnen und Träger. Was Chen gerade jetzt anstrebte, war das Mögliche als beherrschendes Element. Aus diesem Grund machte er das Theater – und speziell die Stücke Shakespeares mit ihrem ausgelassenen Spiel der persönlichen Identitäten – zur Prämisse seiner Arbeit. Die Bühne selbst bietet sich als Hauptmetapher an. Chens Schmuckstücke verhalten sich genauso wie „alle Frau'n und Männer [als] bloße Spieler" in *Wie es euch gefällt:* Sie „treten auf und gehen wieder ab". Sie spielen die *Idee* von Raum durch, anstatt ihn nur abzubilden. Einzelne Motive innerhalb der Stücke dienen weitgehend demselben Zweck, den in einer modernen Bühnenproduktion die Requisiten übernehmen, indem sie für jede Interpretation offen sind (wie etwa jene, die Isamu Noguchi für die Choreografin Martha Graham entwarf). Ein amorpher Streifen Grasgrün lässt sich als Olivenbaum, Flusslauf oder Algenbeet deuten, ein blau-weißer Fleck als Meereswoge oder zerbrochenes Stück Porzellan. Auch der Maßstab ist ungewiss, sodass ein und dieselbe Arbeit einen Klumpen Erde oder ein ganzes Gebirge andeuten könnte.

Drehen Sie eines dieser Stücke um, und das Gefühl einer Metamorphose ist augenblicklich dahin. Ganz gleich, welche Art von Zauberei auf der Vorderseite stattfinden mag, die Rückseite ist vollkommen unverhüllt, nüchtern, eine praktische Infrastruktur, die untersucht werden will – so als träte man im Theater hinter die Kulissen. (Es könnte relevant sein, dass Chens Vater als Bühnenbildner für israelische Film-, Theater- und Fernsehproduktionen gearbeitet hat.) Diese Recto-Ansichten rufen auch das Frühwerk des zutiefst theateraffinen Künstlers Robert Rauschenberg in Erinnerung, dessen *Combines* der Kunstkritiker Leo Steinberg in denkwürdiger Weise mit dem „Flachbett" einer Druckerpresse verglich, mit einer „Rezeptionsfläche, auf der Objekte verteilt werden, auf der Daten eingegeben werden, auf der Informationen empfangen, gedruckt, eingeprägt werden können – sei es zusammenhängend oder in ungeordneter Form".[3] Diese Beschreibung trifft auch auf Chens Werk zu. Indem er sich vom Konstrukt der Perspektive befreite, ermöglichte er das Einströmen einer anderen Art von Wirklichkeit.

---

3 Leo Steinberg, „Other Criteria: The Flatbed Picture Plane", in: Other Criteria: Confrontations with Twentieth-Century Art, New York 1972, S. 84.
4 Samuel Johnson zitiert nach Boswell's Life of Johnson, Bd. 2: 1776–1784, London et al. 1904, S. 559.

Der Schriftsteller Samuel Johnson bemerkte einst über John Milton, der Shakespeare als herausragender Dichter Englands nachgefolgt war, dieser sei „ein Genie, das aus einem Felsen einen Koloss hauen, aber keine Köpfe in Kirschkerne schnitzen konnte".[4] Bei Chen war es andersherum. Während der Pandemie schuf er zwar ungewöhnlich großformatige Arbeiten – insbesondere eine mehr als drei Meter breite Wandskulptur, die 2022 im Rahmen seiner Ausstellung *Pars Pro Toto* in der Galleria Antonella Villanova im italienischen Foiano della Chiana gezeigt wurde. Doch wie die meisten Goldschmiede verstand er sich im Kern als Miniaturkünstler, als Anhänger einer Kunst der Verdichtung. Eine Untergruppe von Arbeiten aus der Serie *All the World's a Stage*, für die Chen seine älteren, linsenförmigen Kompositionen zu Halbkugeln erweiterte, macht dies besonders deutlich. Die Stücke waren inspiriert von einer weiteren kunsthistorischen Quelle: Gebetsnüsse aus Buchsbaumholz, die im 16. Jahrhundert vor allem in den Niederlanden gefertigt wurden. Es überrascht nicht, dass Chen diese außergewöhnlich komplizierten Schnitzereien bewunderte. Sie sind nicht nur Wunderwerke der Handwerkskunst, sondern zeigen auch, wie viel Raum sich in ein kleines, nichtperspektivisches Objekt zwängen lässt, das in alle Richtungen rotiert wie die Wäsche in einem Trockner. Was besonders überrascht, ist der Eindruck großer Entfernung, den die Bildschnitzer heraufbeschworen, ein Kunstgriff, den auch Chen beherrschte. Wir befinden uns hier im Bereich des Dioramas, in dem die Magie der Darstellung die Aufmerksamkeit sichtbar auf sich selbst lenkt.

Wohin führt uns das alles? Einen Anhaltspunkt dazu liefert eines der Lieblingsbücher Chens, David Hockneys *Geheimes Wissen* (2001), das in unseren Tagen die Kunstgeschichte genauso einflussreich umzuschreiben wusste wie Panofskys „Perspektive als ‚symbolische Form'" in der damaligen Zeit (es lohnt sich, die beiden Texte parallel zu lesen). Hockney führt überzeugend vor Augen, dass Paradigmenwechsel in der Darstellung – wie die plötzliche, faszinierende Wirklichkeitsnähe, die im 17. Jahrhundert in der niederländischen Malerei aufkam – üblicherweise am besten mit verfeinerten optischen Hilfsmitteln zu erklären sind, insbesondere mit verschiedenen Bauformen der Camera obscura und anderen, auf Linsen basierenden Vorrichtungen. (Dass die Anzahl urkundlicher Belege für solche Hilfsmittel relativ gering ist, erklärt Hockney mit der Vermutung, diese seien sorgsam gehütete Betriebsgeheimnisse gewesen, daher auch der Titel seines Buches.) Auch wenn Chen technische Hilfsmittel nicht buchstäblich auf diese Weise verwendete, erscheint der Gedanke absurd, seine Arbeit könnte die Formen annehmen, die sie heute hat, wenn es die in unserer Zeit vorherrschenden digitalen Bedingungen des Sehens nicht gäbe. Computer sehen, ohne tatsächlich hinzusehen. Das Internet erzeugt die Illusion, alle beliebigen Bezugspunkte seien auf der Stelle verfügbar, beraubt sie jedoch gleichzeitig jeglichen Zusammenhangs. Wie die Künstlerin und Kunsttheoretikerin Hito Steyerl 2011 in ihrem Essay „In Free Fall" feststellte, einer postmodernen Antwort auf Panofskys Argumentation, wird der „stabile und einzelne Blickwinkel [...] ergänzt (und häufig ersetzt) durch multiple Perspektiven, sich überlappende Fenster, verzerrte Fluchtlinien und divergierende Fluchtpunkte".[5]

Attai Chen setzte einen Kontrapunkt zu diesem zersplitterten, endlosen Meer von unbedeutenden Bildern. Er reagierte auf die Gegenwart, die scheinbar reibungsfrei dahinfließt, diese omnipräsente Ablenkungsmaschine, in der für uns Wahrheit und Lüge nicht mehr zu unterscheiden sind, mit seinen eigenen, ebenso fließenden, aber kunstvoll gefertigten Mikrokosmen. Sie sind „Erfindungen" in jedem Sinne des Wortes: Aus dem Nichts entstanden, machen sie nicht nur Eindruck, sondern wirken dabei auch noch betont greifbar und vollkommen flüchtig zugleich. Halten Sie eines dieser Stücke in der Hand und betrachten Sie es genau: Was Sie sehen werden, ist eine ganz andere Welt als Ihre eigene, die diese gleichwohl vollständig umfasst.

5 Hito Steyerl, „In Free Fall," e-flux Journal 24 (April 2011), https://www.e-flux.com/journal/24/67860/in-free-fall-a-thought-experiment-on-vertical-perspective/

Sool Park
CORDYCEPS

Noch einmal geboren werden, und dafür das jetzige Leben hingeben – das ist die alte Formel der Unsterblichkeit. Bei näherem Hinsehen ist die Natur voll mit unsterblichen Wesen, ja es scheint sogar unmöglich, in ihr ein normal Sterbliches auszumachen. Ein Leib, der einst sich hin und her bewegte auf dem Waldboden, kommt zum Stillstand, um sich neu zu gebären. Ganz unerwartet und wundervoll wird er aber durch ein Fremdes beseelt, das ihm das alte Leben kostet; in diesem Übergang schmückt und erneuert er sich – und ist schon ein anderer – wer also stirbt in diesem Leib, wer lebt? Diese Frage gilt auch uns, die wir doch auch einen Leib beseelen und ständig im Werden hausen müssen, wie Gäste in einem Traum.

Sool Park
STILLE UNTERGÄNGE, IMMER AUFSTEIGENDE BLICKE

UNS ÜBERFÜLLTS. WIR ORDNENS. ES ZERFÄLLT.
WIR ORDNENS WIEDER UND ZERFALLEN SELBST.
Rainer Maria Rilke, Duineser Elegien (8. Elegie)

Unser Auge bricht das Licht, wie jedes optische Medium. Was wir sehen, ist demnach immer schon das Gebrochene, nie die ganze Wirklichkeit. Ja, Sehen ist Brechen, das ist die alte Grundprämisse der modernen Philosophie: und die große Rede davon, dass wir nur Bilder von Dingen haben, nie die Dinge selbst. Was die Philosophen selbst produzierten, sind allerdings auch nur Bilder, nämlich von der Welt. Während jedoch die ermüdete Philosophie langsam aufhört, frische Weltbilder zu entwerfen, scheinen Künstler nun die besseren Philosophen zu sein. Unbewusst meist schimmern in den gelungenen Arbeiten Ideen durch, die unser Inneres begreifen und zur neuen Sichtbarkeit zwingen. In diesem Sinne ist Kunstwerk „Modell der Wirklichkeit"[1], oder Miniatur der Welt.

In Attai Chens neuen Arbeiten haben wir zwei konkurrierende Modelle des Sehens: zwei Weltbilder, die sich gegenüberstehen oder zwei Arten von Bühnen, könnte man sagen. Das eine Weltbild *(Dioramas)* ist zentrifugal, es zeugt von Bruch; das andere *(Prayer Nuts)* träumt hingegen von konzentrischer Ganzheit und Regeneration. Ist es Widerstreit zwischen ihnen, oder ein kompensatorisches Verhältnis? Es scheint, dass hier beides der Fall ist – so wie sich Licht und Dunkel gegenseitig verneinen und doch nur zwei Seiten *einer* Sache sind. Auch Nietzsche schreibt ja von einem heilenden Licht, das demjenigen erscheint, der zu tief in den Abgrund geschaut hat.[2] So rufen die beiden Weltbilder einander hervor, wie Träume nacheinander erscheinen, sich gegenseitig deuten und zugleich verwirren.

Dioramas: Die Welt als Bühne

Diorama heißt wörtlich ‚durchschauen'. Ein Diorama schaut also in die Tiefe, und ordnet dem aktuellen Geschehen ein Bühnenbild im Hintergrund zu. In Attai Chens *Dioramas*-Arbeiten scheint diese Relation zwischen Vorder- und Hintergrund jedoch in eine seltsame Umkehrung zu geraten. In *Untitled*, S. 70 ist das vordergründige Geschehen auf dem Wasser (eine Seenotszene?) fast unerkennbar, ja bedeutungslos; dagegen ragen die Elemente im Hintergrund übertrieben in die Höhe, in eine fantastische Überwucherung. Das Individuum ertrinkt lautlos, während die Welt ins Wanken gerät. Gefährdet ist nicht nur die quasi-architektoni-

---

1 Ludwig Wittgenstein, *Tractatus Logico-Philosophicus*, 2.12.
2 Friedrich Nietzsche, *Kritische Studienausgabe (Geburt der Tragödie)*, Bd. 1, S. 65.

sche Struktur, die an der eigenen Konstruktion scheitert, sondern die ganze Realität: Die hinterste Ebene ist ein Weltenbrand. Es ist eine Miniaturszene unserer aktuellen Weltlage, wo alles zerfällt, brennt oder versinkt. In dieser Szene ist aber eine eigentümliche, tiefe Stille. Ist das die Hilflosigkeit gegenüber dem Weltenlauf, die wir gerade schmerzhaft erlernen müssen? Ist das die neue Gleichgültigkeit?

Dieses Muster des stillen Aus-den-Fugen-Geratens durchzieht die ganze *Dioramas*-Serie. Kennzeichnend bleibt die Unmöglichkeit der Stabilität, das wiederkehrende Sprengen des eigenen Formats. Scheinbare Naturszenen wie *Untitled*, S. 51 verbergen unheimliche Ahnungen; die Plastizität der Rauchwolke macht sie nicht weniger bedrohlich, sondern zeigt nunmehr den Bühnencharakter des Vorgangs auf. „Die ganze Welt ist [eine] Bühne", wie Shakespeare in *Wie es euch gefällt* schreibt,[3] und wir verstehen plötzlich, was hier gerade im Untergang begriffen ist – nämlich die Bühnenhaftigkeit von Welt. Die Fassaden entlarven sich als falsche Wände, die ein Bühnenbildner aufgestellt hat, man ertappt den Souffleur bei der Arbeit. Der alte Verdacht bestätigt sich. Ist es Freiheit? Oder Unmöglichkeit?

Prayer Nuts: Die zweite Welt

Die Idee hinter der mittelalterlichen Erfindung der Gebetsnuss war es wohl, einen tragbaren Kosmos zu erschaffen. Attai Chens Serie *Prayer Nuts* ist eine künstlerische Fortführung dieser uralten Idee, einen inneren Zufluchtsort zu materialisieren, entgegen dem Auseinanderfallen von Sinn. Sie hebt das Nirgends und Niemand der äußeren Welt auf und versucht, „die Welt im Innersten zusammenzuhalten"[4]. Die Bestandteile bleiben die architektonischen und geografischen Elemente in Miniatur, wie in den *Dioramas*-Arbeiten; auch das Bedrohliche lebt fort, die Strukturen sind brüchig, zerrüttet, verkohlt und auf jeden Fall verlassen, auch dort, wo sie unerwartet golden aufglänzen. Doch alle diese wüsten Landschaften sind sphärisch um die Mitte geordnet, man sieht sogar die materialisierte Himmelsdecke, ein typisches Merkmal religiöser Vorstellungswelten. Die optische Perspektive ist aus der Betrachtung verschwunden, denn die Wirklichkeit selbst wird hier verbogen, um ein abgeschlossenes, begrenztes Ganzes zu bilden. Hier ist eine mystische Welt,[5] aber zugleich eine Welt, wie wir sie tatsächlich um uns wahrnehmen. In *Untitled*, S. 89 sehen wir einen wohlgeordneten Bau, der dennoch unbewohnbar und unbewohnt ist. Halb an Himmel, halb an Hölle erinnernd, kann dieser als eine Nachempfindung der Kohärenz widersprüchlicher Seelenzustände gelesen werden. Die Elemente in *Untitled*, S. 93/r sind wiederum unmögliche Konstruktionen und entlarvte Fassaden, doch sie sind sicher in die konzentrische Sphäre integriert; denn es gibt hier Schwerkraft, die Halt gibt. Eine wesentliche Eigenschaft dieser Mikrokosmen ist ihr Charakter als *zweite Welten*. In ihnen erreichen Dinge die ersehnte Ganzheit, selbst wenn sie von Trauer und Verlust gezeichnet ist, wie in *Untitled*, S. 93/l. In *Untitled*, S. 86/r, S. 87 scheint uns dann aber eine verklärte Sicht auf, als magischer Moment der Regeneration.

Aber diese Gegenwelten von Attai Chen sind mehr als Weltbilder, denn sie sind als Schmuckstücke gemeint. Als solche sind sie gedacht, am eigenen Körper getragen, gefühlt und mitgeteilt zu werden. Könnte man mit Ilse Aichinger sagen, ihre Funktion sei es, „die Untergänge vor sich her [zu] schleifen"?[6] Denn es sind stille Bilder des Untergangs, die uns einen Schritt voraus gehen und etwas Dunkles sagen. Wir sehen darin, dass wir mit unserem Sehen die Welt gebrochen haben. Wir sehen aber auch, dass es damit nicht zu Ende ist. Denn aufwärts gehen unsere Blicke, bis sie die blaue Himmelsdecke fassen.

---

3 Shakespeare, Wie es euch gefällt, Akt 2, Szene 7. Engl.: „All the world's a stage."
4 Johann Wolfgang von Goethe, „Nachts", in: Faust. Der Tragödie erster Teil.
5 Ludwig Wittgenstein, Tractatus Logico-Philosophicus, 6.45: „Das Gefühl der Welt als ein begrenztes Ganzes ist das mystische."
6 Ilse Aichinger, Schlechte Wörter, Frankfurt/Main 1976, S. 8.

Attai Chen
CV

1979 Born in Jerusalem, Israel
2023 Died in Munich, Germany

EDUCATION

2007–2012 Diploma with honors ("Meisterschüler"), Prof. Otto Künzli Class for Jewellery and Objects, Academy of Fine Arts, Munich (DE)
2002–2006 B.F.A, Dep. of Jewellery and Fashion, Bezalel Academy of Arts and Design, Jerusalem (IL)

SOLO & TWO PERSON EXHIBITIONS

2022 "Territories of Imperfection," Beseder Gallery, curated by Hagai Segev, Prague (CZ)
2021 "Pars Pro Toto," Gallery Antonella Villanova, curated by Emanuela Nobile Mino, Foiano (IT)
"Interflow," with Kim Su Jin and Fuse, Lakeville, Shanghai (CN)
2020 "Eine Frage der Verwandlung," with Mirjam Hiller, Gallery Slavik, Vienna (AT)
2019 Athens Jewellery Week Guest Artist, curated by Anticlastic, Benaki Museum, Athens (GR)
2018 "Morphogenesis," with Carina Shoshtary, Gallery LA Joaillerie par Mazlo, curated by Céline Robin, Paris (FR)
"Mirjam Hiller + Attai Chen," Gallery Reverso, Lisbon (PT)
"Matter in Perspective," Gallery RA, Amsterdam (NL)
"In Motion," FROOTS Gallery, Beijing (CN)
"Echoes of Order," with Carina Shoshtary, ATTA Gallery, Bangkok (TH)
"arnoldsche weekend gallery #6," with Johannes Nagel, arnoldsche Art Publishers, Stuttgart (DE)
2017 "Micromania," with Carina Shoshtary, FROOTS Gallery, Shanghai (CN)
2016 "Matter of Perspective," Gallery Loupe, Montclair, New Jersey (US)
2015 "Terra Mutantica," Gallery Loupe, Montclair, New Jersey (US)
"Terra Mutantica," Gallery Spektrum, Munich (DE)
2014 Four Gallery, Gothenburg (SE)
"In Between," Tel Aviv Museum of Art (IL)
"Cross Breeding," with Carina Shoshtary, Gallery RA, Amsterdam (NL)
2013 "Compounding Fractions," Gallery Loupe, Montclair, New Jersey (US)
2012 "Cycle of Mishaps," with Vered Kaminsky, Gallery RA, Amsterdam (NL)
"Betz-Chen," with Doris Betz, Gallery Spektrum, Munich (DE)

AWARDS AND SCHOLARSHIPS

Since 2021 Artist Studio Grant of the Bavarian Cultural Council (DE)
2017 18th Artist Award of the City of Fürstenfeldbruck (DE)
Artist-in-residence at Konstepidemin (SE)
2014–2020 Artist Studio Grant, from the city of Munich (DE)
2014, 2016 Nominee for the Munich Art and Design Awards (DE)
2014 Finalist at the AJF Artist Awards (US)
Andrea M. Bronfman Prize for the Arts (IL)
2012 Oberbayerischer Förderpreis für Angewandte Kunst (DE)
2011 STIBET Grant (DE)
Herbert-Hofmann-Preis (DE)

2008–2010	DAAD scholarship (DE)
2006	Lokman Award for Applied Arts (IL)
	Schneidinger Foundation-Grant (IL)
2005–2006	America-Israel Cultural Foundation Scholarship (IL)
2005	Romi Shapira Prize for Judaica (IL)

TEACHING EXPERIENCE / LECTURES (SELECTION)

Since 2019	Teaching, Dep. of Jewellery and Fashion, Bezalel Academy of Arts and Design, Jerusalem (IL)
2019	Lecture, "There and Back Again: A Journey with Jewelry," Athens Jewelry Week (GR)
	Workshop, School of Design and Crafts, Gothenburg (SE)
2017	Workshop, China University of Geosciences, Dep. of Jewellery, Wuhan, Hubei (CN)
	Workshop, Penland School of Crafts, North Carolina (US)
	Teaching, Rhode Island School of Design, Providence, Rhode Island (US)
2016–2019	Guest teacher, Alchimia Contemporary Jewellery School, Florence (IT)
2016	Workshop/lecture, Cranbrook Academy of Art, Bloomfield Hills, Michigan (US)
2014	Lecture, School of Design and Crafts, Gothenburg (SE)
2013	Workshop, Master in Design, Shenkar College of Engineering, Design and Art, Ramat Gan (IL)
	Lecture, Brooklyn Metal Works, New York City, New York (US)
	Lecture, University of Applied Sciences, Munich (US)
2012–2014	Teaching, Dep. of Jewellery and Fashion, Bezalel Academy of Arts and Design, Jerusalem (IL)
Since 2011	Teaching, Jewellery Techniques, Volkshochschule, Munich (DE)
2011	Lecture, SACRILEGIUM 2.0, 43rd Jewellery Symposium, Zimmerhof (DE)
2007	Lecture, Jewelry Design Dep., Shenkar College of Engineering, Art and Design, Ramat Gan (IL)
2005–2007	Assistant lecturer, Dep. of Jewellery and Fashion, Bezalel Academy of Arts and Design, Jerusalem (IL)

WORK IN PUBLIC COLLECTIONS (SELECTION)

Alice & Louis Koch Ring Collection, Schweizerisches Nationalmuseum/Landesmuseum Zürich (CH)
Arkansas Arts Centre, Little Rock, Arkansas (US)
CODA Museum, Apeldoorn (NL)
The Donna Schneier Collection, Metropolitan Museum of Art, New York City, New York (US)
Helen Williams Drutt Family Collection, Philadelphia (US)
KOLUMBA – Kunstmuseum des Erzbistums Köln (DE)
The Museum of Fine Arts, Houston, Texas (US)
MAD – Museum of Arts and Design, New York City, New York (US)
Die Neue Sammlung – The Design Museum at Pinakothek der Moderne, Munich (DE)
The Israel Museum, Jerusalem (IL)
Schmuckmuseum Pforzheim (DE)
Rotasa Collection Trust, San Francisco, California (US)
Sanford and Susan Kempin Collection, New York City, New York (US)
Susan Grant Lewin Collection, Cooper Hewitt, Smithsonian Design Museum, New York City, New York (US)
Tel Aviv Museum of Art (IL)

ACKNOWLEDGEMENTS

Our deepest gratitude goes to everyone who helped in the realization of the project, especially **the artist's family** and the individuals who generously offered their advice, creativity, and support throughout its creation.

Special thanks to the following contributors:
Bonnie Levine, Catherine Rose, Deedie Potter Rose, Erwin und Gisela von Steiner-Stiftung, FROOTS Gallery, Gail Hufjay, Galleria Antonella Villanova, Gallery Loupe, Jennifer Altmann, Karen and Michael Rotenberg, Linda Peshkin, Rotasa Fund, and Susan Kempin.

Fiscal sponsorship: Art Jewelry Forum

IMPRINT

© 2024 CARINA SHOSHTARY, THE AUTHORS AND ARNOLDSCHE ART PUBLISHERS, STUTTGART

All rights reserved. No part of this work may be reproduced or used in any form or by any means without written permission from the copyright holders.
www.arnoldsche.com

EDITOR
Carina Shoshtary

AUTHORS
Glenn Adamson
Sool Park

TRANSLATIONS
Joan Clough, Castallack
Dr. Kurt Rehkopf, Hamburg

COPYEDITING
Wendy Brouwer, Stuttgart

GRAPHIC DESIGNER
Tanja Kischel, Munich

OFFSET REPRODUCTIONS
Paladin Design- und Werbemanufaktur, Remseck

PRINTED BY
Schleunungdruck, Marktheidenfeld

PAPER
140 g/m² Magno Natural

PROJECT COORDINATION ARNOLDSCHE
Julia Hohrein

PROJECT ADVISOR
Patti Bleicher, director, Gallery Loupe

PHOTO CREDITS
Attai Chen, Munich
Mirei Takeuchi, Munich

COVER ILLUSTRATION
Attai Chen, Untitled | Drawing | 2022 | Cardboard, acrylic, pencil | 250 × 175 mm

Aus Gründen der besseren Lesbarkeit verwenden wir das generische Maskulinum. Wir meinen stets alle Geschlechter im Sinne der Gleichbehandlung. Die verkürzte Sprachform hat redaktionelle Gründe und ist wertfrei.

Bibliographic information published by the Deutsche Nationalbibliothek. The Deutsche Nationalbibliothek lists this publication in the Deutsche Nationalbibliografie; detailed bibliographic data are available at www.dnb.de

ISBN 978-3-89790-720-1

Made in Germany, 2024

This book has been produced with the generous support of